A SERIES FOR THE FANS

WOODFORD PRESS, *San Francisco*
Produced in partnership with
MAJOR LEAGUE BASEBALL PROPERTIES, INC.

AN OFFICIAL PUBLICATION OF MAJOR
LEAGUE BASEBALL

A SERIES
FOR
THE FANS

Contents

This *Official Book of the 1995 World Series* was made possible by the generous assistance of The New Era Cap Company, Inc., Authentic Diamond Collection licensee of Major League Baseball Properties and suppliers of the official 1995 World Series Championship Clubhouse cap.

WOODFORD PRESS
660 Market Street, San Francisco, CA 94104

Book design by Laurence J. Hyman

Produced in partnership with and licensed by
MAJOR LEAGUE BASEBALL PROPERTIES, INC.

ISBN: 0-942627-22-9
Library of Congress Catalog Number applied for
First Printing: November 1995
Printed and bound in the United States of America

A SERIES FOR THE FANS

By Ron Fimrite

THERE WERE CRITICAL ELEMENTS in the 1995 World Series that could well have stretched the tension level beyond the breaking point. Here were two cities desperate for a championship. Cleveland had not had a team in the Series in 41 years, had not had a Series winner in 47 years. Atlanta had never before had a champion in any major professional sport and had endured the additional frustration of losing two of the last three Series. Here also was a national sporting public, disillusioned by baseball's ongoing labor difficulties, looking on anxiously, some might even say querulously, at the resumption of Series play after last year's cancellation. And here was the game itself, eager to put on a show that would restore it in the public eye as the once and forever National Pastime.

"Just thinking about such things," said Atlanta's Tom Glavine, "is enough to drive you crazy."

But Glavine's sanity, as we shall see, was never threatened and, with pressure on them as never before, baseball's two best teams put on an unforgettable show. Five of the six games were decided by a single run, including one heart-pounding extra-inning affair and an equally gripping finale. There were two pitching performances that must rank among the finest in World Series history. There were gaffes and pratfalls and some amazing plays afield. There were tape-measure home runs. There was daring base running and outright foolish base running. There was, in brief, a little bit of everything. And that's the way it should be in what yet remains, in a year of restoration, redemption and renaissance, the Fall Classic.

Just getting to this Series was a more demanding ordeal than ever before, the two teams having been obliged to hurdle an additional round of playoffs before facing off for their respective league championships. But through all of these taxing preliminary games—nine for Cleveland, eight for Atlanta—the teams with the best regular season records in baseball—100-44 for Cleveland, 90-54 for Atlanta—emerged unscathed.

The Indians, in fact, appeared to be a team for the ages. Their collective batting average of .291 was the highest in the major leagues since the Boston Red Sox hit .302 in 1950. They led the majors in runs scored with 840 and home runs with 207. And they also led the American League with a pitching staff ERA of 3.83. But pitching has long been the Braves' strong suit and behind Greg Maddux's remarkable 19-2 won-loss record and 1.63 ERA, they led the majors with a staff ERA of 3.44. And pitching, inevitably, would decide this fiercely contested Series.

It certainly decided the opening game in Atlanta as Maddux fashioned a near masterpiece, a complete game two-hitter. Both of the Indians' runs in this 3-2 Braves victory were unearned, the first coming when tiny (5-foot-6) Rafael Belliard, playing shortstop in place of the injured Jeff Blauser, bobbled a ground ball hit to him by the game's leadoff hitter, Kenny Lofton. A swashbuckler on the base paths, Lofton then stole second and third and scored on Carlos Baerga's infield out. The Braves tied the score in the second on Fred McGriff's long home run, and the two teams remained deadlocked until the seventh, when Indians starter Orel Hershiser, who had been breezing along on a three-hitter (with seven strikeouts), unaccountably walked the first two batters, McGriff and Dave Justice.

There followed a most unusual discussion on the mound between Hershiser (who, at 37, looks more like a graduate student in chemical engineering than a major league star) and his pitching coach, Mark Wiley. Hershiser was arguing, successfully, as it turns out, to have himself removed from the game. This from a man nicknamed "Bulldog." A satisfactory explanation for this self-imposed hook was not forthcoming until the next day, when Hershiser revealed that he had simply lost his "release point"—the spot in midair where a pitcher lets go of the ball—and was fearful that without it he might untie the score with a misguided delivery to the next hitter, the dangerous Ryan Klesko.

And so, shrouded at that time in mystery, Orel trudged to the showers, to be replaced by left-hander Paul Assenmacher, who promptly walked pinch hitter Mike Devereaux to load the bases. That brought in Julian Tavarez, a gaudy 10-2 pitcher in the regular season, who induced Luis Polonia to hit a grounder that shortstop Omar Vizquel juggled, but was given credit for a force at second base by umpire Bruce Froemming. McGriff scored the go-ahead run on the play. And a squeeze play brought Justice home for 3-1. The Indians would get their second unearned run in the ninth, but to no avail.

On just 95 pitches, Maddux had shut down baseball's most potent offense. He walked no one, and the only hits he permitted were softly-stroked opposite-field singles by left-hand hitters Lofton and Jim Thome. "It just seemed typical of him to me," said catcher Charlie O'Brien of Maddux's performance. "This is something we've come to expect from him." For Hershiser it would be his first Post Season loss after a record seven straight wins.

In Game Two, Glavine was not quite up to such brilliance—that would come

Greg Maddux was his usual self in Game One—brilliant.

Orel Hershiser suffered his first Post Season loss in Game One.

later—but he did give the Braves six serviceable innings in a 4-3 win. The Indians again took an early lead when 39-year-old Eddie Murray, compelled by Series rules to play first base in the National League park instead of the more sedentary designated hitter, walloped a two-run second-inning homer. The Braves tied the score in the third and then went inexorably ahead in the sixth on a two-run homer off Dennis Martinez by catcher Javier Lopez. Justice had singled ahead of him and gone to second when Belle, a mighty slugger but an indifferent fielder, fumbled the ball on the bounce for an error. The Indians got one run back in the seventh and had the tying run on base with one out in the eighth when Ramirez took a gambling lead off first. McGriff took note of this and so advised catcher Lopez. So when Ramirez strayed too far on the next pitch, Lopez fired to first for the pickoff. Ramirez left the field shaking his head in contrition.

The teams now moved to Cleveland, where the Indians hadn't won a Series game since Oct. 9, 1948. They would eventually win that year—prophetically?—over the Braves, then representing Boston, as they later would Milwaukee, before finally settling in Atlanta. This Tuesday night Series game would be the first played in Cleveland's new Jacobs Field, a facility, like those also newly built in Baltimore, Denver and Arlington, Tex., that combines fin de siecle amenities with traditional pre-1960s ballpark architecture. Jacobs is a joy to behold. It has a field of natural grass (as does Atlanta's Fulton County Stadium). It has the look and feel of classic ballparks like Fenway and Wrigley, only it's spiffier and, with an active public address system, louder. Jacobs is all shadowy green and white and when flashbulbs sparkle like fireflies in the darkened stands, it calls to mind warm summer evenings in the park.

Unfortunately, there was nothing at all warm about the evening of Oct. 24, 1995. The game-time temperature was 49 degrees, but with a 23-mile-an-hour gale blowing in toward right field off Lake Erie, the wind-chill factor was a teeth-chattering 29 degrees. Who knows how cold it was when this 11-inning, four-hour-and-nine-minute struggle abated? And for the cheering, placard-bearing Cleveland fans, thirsting for victory after a 47-year drought, who cared?

The Cleveland players seemed equally oblivious to the cold. Down two games to none, they held a pre-game pep rally in the clubhouse. "If we're going down," an emotional Sandy Alomar told his teammates, "we'll go down fighting and with dignity." Belle was so unsettled by the two losses that he took some of his rage out on a TV reporter who was in the dugout, legitimately, awaiting an interview with Lofton. She picked the right man, as it developed, for Lofton was the spark the Indians needed this night, banging out three hits, walking three times, scoring three runs, stealing a base and making several fine catches in center field.

The Indians banished Braves starter John Smoltz in the third inning, moving out to a 4-1 lead. The Jacobs Field P.A. system, which leads the major leagues in decibel count, serenaded the departing pitcher with a version of "Hit the Road, Jack" that shattered glassware as far away as Halifax, Nova Scotia, and set toes a-tapping aboard a cruise ship off the coast of Barbados.

But the Braves were far from finished. Homers by McGriff in the sixth and Klesko in the seventh made it 4-3. Another Lofton run upped the lead to 5-3 in the Indians' half of the seventh. And then in the eighth, the Braves scored three to take a 6-5 lead that might have been even greater had Lofton not snared McGriff's prodigious drive to dead center with an over-the-shoulder catch. And then . . . what a

"They didn't win 100 games for nothing. They can play. But we feel if we play our best baseball we can win."
—*David Justice*

The Series moved to chilly Jacobs Field for Game Three.

game! . . . the Indians came back again to tie the game in their half of the eighth when Alomar doubled Ramirez home. The shivering crowd was now in a frenzy, stomping in time to a sound system rendition of "We Will Rock You."

The Braves threatened again in the ninth when, with runners on second and third, Herbert Perry, in as a defensive replacement at first base, made a gorgeous scoop of Chipper Jones' line shot to end the inning. It was "the play of the game," said Manager Mike Hargrove. The game had by now resolved itself into an improbable duel between the Braves' Mark Wohlers and the Indians' Jose Mesa, two "closers" who are rarely asked to go more than one inning, that usually being the ninth, and with their team in the lead. But this game didn't seem to have a last inning and no one stayed in the lead for long.

So Wohlers and Mesa, specialists in near-100-mile-an-hour fastballs, labored in stalemate. Hargrove, knowing his team faced virtual extinction, could not risk removing a reliever who had led both leagues with 46 saves and Atlanta Manager Bobby Cox, anxious to tighten the noose, wanted his best in at the finish.

Cox was the first to blink, lifting Wohlers after two-and-two-thirds innings in favor of Pena opening the 11th. The first batter Pena faced, Baerga, doubled off the wall in center field. Alvaro Espinoza was summoned to run for him, Baerga having injured his right ankle in Game One. Belle, the first player ever to hit 50 doubles and 50 homers in the same season, was walked intentionally. And then Murray lined a single to right, Espinoza crossing the plate with the winning run as the ecstatic crowd bellowed its pleasure and the P.A. played a Bruce Springsteen number, "Glory Days," that broke a bathroom window in the home of a Mrs. Tully in Daly City, California.

Mesa, who pitched the final three innings to earn the win, hadn't pitched that long since the first week of the season. "I feel strong," he said afterward. "I'm ready to go again."

"If you didn't think this was an unbelievable baseball game," said Wohlers, "you're not a fan. This is the kind of game that will make people fall in love with baseball all over again."

It was also the kind of game that saved the Indians from tumbling into an 0-3 abyss, from which no team in World Series history had ever emerged. A win now in Game Four would even the Series and with Game Five also to be played in Cleveland there was sound hope for a turnaround. Ken Hill, acquired in July from St. Louis and a shutout pitcher in the ALCS, was Hargrove's pick for this pivotal fourth game. Cox, refusing to pitch Maddux out of turn, called on left-hander Steve Avery, who, with a 7-13 record, was the only Braves starter with a losing record in the regular season. But Avery had pitched six shutout innings in the final game of the NLCS.

Neither starter allowed a run through the first five innings of this second game in Cleveland. Then in the sixth inning, the teams traded homers, Klesko for the Braves, Belle for the Indians. But Hill came a cropper in the seventh, giving up a go-ahead run on a Polonia double before being replaced by Assenmacher, brought in specifically to deal with lefty sluggers McGriff and Justice. He struck out McGriff, but Justice foiled the strategy with a two-run single that moved the Braves ahead, 4-1. This three-run inning would prove sufficient, although another run was added in the ninth when left-fielder Belle collapsed like a lawn chair futilely pursuing McGriff's blooper and Lopez doubled the run home. A Ramirez homer in the ninth would make the final score 5-2.

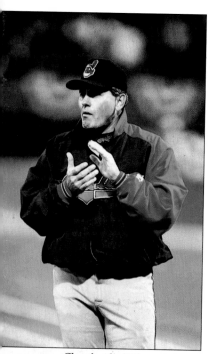

Cleveland's Mike Hargrove directed the American League's most potent lineup.

Kenny Lofton's skills made him a scoring threat every time he stepped to the plate.

The Indians were now down three games to one, and of the 39 previous Series teams in that unenviable position, 36 had lost. And for good measure, the opposing pitcher in Game Five would be the apparently unbeatable Maddux. "I'd be lying if I said we didn't feel the pressure," Indians first-sacker Paul Sorrento said of his team's bleak prospects. "We're one game from elimination. But we've ripped off 10-15 games in a row during the season (actually, their longest was nine in a row). And this would be a nice time to start one of those streaks."

Avery, who gave up only one run and three hits in his six innings, was humble in victory. "I am honored," he said, "to be a part of what may go down as one of the great pitching staffs of all time."

So now it was up to Maddux to pitch the clincher. He accepted the assignment with his customary aplomb. In fact, it is difficult to conceive of any situation sufficiently hair-raising to ruffle this unflappable young player. The night before the fifth game, he slept his usual ten hours, showed up at the ballpark with his usual five-o'clock shadow and all but snoozed away the hours before game time.

Steve Avery's Game Four outing gave Atlanta a 3-1 advantage.

The pressure was really on Hershiser in this fifth game. Not only did he represent the last barrier between his team and a long winter of regret, he was also under some compulsion to make amends for his hasty leave-taking in Game One. He may well have done the right thing by removing himself—taking one for the team, as it were—but such occurrences are exceedingly rare, particularly in a World Series where pitchers generally carry on until they drop from exhaustion or disabling injury. Hershiser's departure was occasioned by nothing more debilitating than technical difficulties. Now, he had to prove he was made of the right stuff.

Although the odds were overwhelmingly against the Indians, there were no symptoms of despair inside raucous Jacobs Field this fateful night. The fans, who routinely rose to cheer on every two-strike count, were now cheering loudly even before the game, this despite a sudden rainstorm that canceled batting practice. The ever-present placards certainly betrayed no suggestion of defeatism: "Nobody's Gonna Steal Our Dream," "There is no Fat Lady in Cleveland." And the sound system still propelled to distant parts tunes apparently selected for their volume potential from the archives of the nearby Rock 'n' Roll Hall of Fame.

Tony Pena's leg pad offers comfort and greetings.

It was Hargrove's 46th birthday, and he was counting on his pitcher for the appropriate gift. "If you have to go into a game like this," he said, "Orel Hershiser definitely fills the bill." That he did. The bulldog was back. He went eight strong innings, allowed only five hits, struck out six and gave up only one earned run, a rare homer off the bat of the diminutive Polonia. A second run scored courtesy of a throwing error by Hershiser himself. The Indians, meanwhile, scored two in the first on Belle's homer to right, two more in the sixth on run-scoring singles by Thome and Ramirez and a final run in the eighth on a tremendous 436-foot homer to right center by Thome. Thome is a congenial and modest young man, but he is a menacing figure at the plate who, as he assumes his stance, points his bat as if it were a rapier aimed at the heart of the opposing pitcher. It didn't seem so at the time, but his homer would prove to be the winning run, since Klesko hit another, his third in three games, that scored two runs in the ninth off Hershiser-successor Mesa. But Mesa recovered in time to strike out Mark Lemke to end the game and give his team a vital 5-4 win.

Jim Thome's Game Five home run was a titanic blast.

This game also established, contrary to all prior evidence, that Maddux was not invincible. He lasted seven innings and gave up four runs on seven hits and, for him, an unconscionable three walks. And he nearly started a riot when, following Belle's two-run homer in the first, he fired a fast ball under Murray's stubbled chin. Eddie, who even in the happiest of circumstances looks disgruntled, first glowered at plate umpire Frank Pulli for permitting such an outrage and then started toward Maddux with catcher O'Brien in earnest pursuit. The two benches emptied and the usual sort of baseball milling about ensued.

But in the confusion there occurred a most unusual confrontation. Hershiser himself had hurried out to the mound to seek an explanation from his opposite number. "Were you throwing at him?" he asked Maddux.

"No," was the reply, "I was just trying to jam him."

"Well, you can do better than that," Hershiser said reproachfully. "Remember, I'm going to have the ball, too." And then these two mild-looking souls separated, exchanging, as Hershiser recalled, "respectful glances." Both agreed that it is rare, indeed, when, in the course of a game, the starting pitchers have an opportunity to exchange differing viewpoints.

With this back-to-the-wall win, the Indians had renewed hope. The fat lady had not sung in Cleveland. Not that anyone would have heard her above the usual din.

But, as Hargrove ruefully acknowledged, "we're still in a hole." They were also back in Atlanta for Game Six, deprived now of the DH and of the tumultuous support of their fans. Those noisy Clevelanders made such an impression on at least one Braves player, Justice, that he felt compelled to belittle the comparatively tepid advocacy of his own fans.

"If we don't win, they'll probably burn our houses down," Justice told local reporters. "If we get down 1-0 tonight, they'll probably boo us out of the stadium. You'd have to do something great to get them out of their seats. Shoot, up in Cleveland, they were down three runs in the ninth inning and they were still on their feet."

Justice was dismayed to see his inflammatory and injudicious remarks headlined in the Saturday newspaper. "My stomach was so upset," he said after reading "Justice Takes a Rip at Braves Fans" as the sports page banner, that "I ate only one banana and a half a sandwich all day. Here you are at home and everybody hates you."

Predictably, Justice was booed when his name was announced in the starting lineup and there were no "Tomahawk Chops" for him when he stepped to the plate for the first time in the second inning. And at least one mean-spirited fan in right field held aloft a placard reading, "Jerk Justice—.167," the numbers representing the beleaguered Braves player's batting average going into the game. But Justice's harangue seemed to work both in his and the fans' favor, for they did a plausible imitation of Jacobs Field hysteria and he had the game of his life. Justice walked twice, doubled in the fourth inning and, in the sixth, rocketed a 410-foot homer that would be the only run of a game that would give the city of Atlanta its first World Series champion after years of near-misses. Immediately after the homer, hit off Georgia Tech alumnus Jim Poole, a new sign appeared in the right field stands: "We're Here for Ya, Davey."

But the real hero of this taut game, and the Series' Most Valuable Player, was Glavine, who pitched a one-hit shutout with eight strikeouts in eight innings. He gave way to exhaustion after eight and turned the last inning over to Wohlers, who

Orel Hershiser and Greg Maddux had a strange meeting in Game Five.

Booed prior to Game Six, David Justice was a hero after his sixth inning home run.

got the final three outs, the first on a sensational running catch by Belliard of Lofton's foul pop. It was the final indignity for Lofton, who, after getting five hits and scoring six runs in the first three games, went hitless and runless in the final three. The key to victory all along, Glavine had said, was keeping Lofton off the base paths.

Actually, Glavine kept almost everyone off the base paths in this pitching gem. The only Cleveland hit was a harmless blooper to center in the sixth by catcher Tony Pena. He walked Belle twice leading off, but the surly slugger was caught stealing the first time and forced at second the next time. Glavine also walked Murray with two outs in the seventh. Cox said he wouldn't have taken his starter out of the game "even if Sandy Koufax was throwing in my bullpen." But when the manager asked Glavine how he was feeling after eight innings, the pitcher frankly told him he was "running out of gas." The gas gauge was already near empty in the eighth, an otherwise typical one-two-three inning distinguished only by a Thome drive that Marquis Grissom pulled down at the warning track in center field.

"I had trouble getting loose that inning and I didn't make that many good pitches," Glavine explained afterward. "I wanted to win this game as badly as any in my life, but I felt I had to fight my emotions and keep my ego in check. I believe in being honest with Bobby, and there should never be any hesitation in giving the ball to Wohlers. I went as hard as I could for as long as I could."

Glavine's superlative clincher reaffirmed the baseball adage that good pitching will always beat good hitting. Smothered by a two-hitter in the first game and a one-hitter in the last, the fearsome Indians sluggers scored only 19 runs in the six games and hit a feeble .179. Lofton, after his early splurge, batted a mere .200 for the Series. The power hitters fared no better, Murray hitting .105, Baerga .192, Thome .211, Ramirez .222 and Belle .235.

Led by Grissom's .360 the Braves hit .244 as a team and outhomered the Indians eight to five. Justice picked the right time to snap out of his Series slump, cracking out his only two extra base hits in the final game and effectively silencing the boos that accompanied his first appearances on the field. He was as exuberant after the game as he was downcast and defensive beforehand. "I wanted the fans to prove me wrong tonight, and they did," he said in the champagne-soaked Braves clubhouse. "It's my own fault for saying what I did, and I admit it."

He had redeemed himself, as had Cox, the losing manager in his team's first two tries at the trophy, but also, as general manager in the late 1980s, the architect of its future. "I never thought of this team as a loser," he said, brushing the suds from his tousled hair. "And I never thought that you had to win a World Series to be called a good manager."

It doesn't hurt your reputation to win one, though. And Bobby Cox is assuredly a winner. And so is the city of Atlanta at long last. Maybe MVP Glavine said it best: "I can say now with a lot of confidence that this is the best team in baseball."

He sure can.

Series MVP Tom Glavine finished off the Indians with his Game Six one-hit masterpiece.

Manager Bobby Cox brought a Series Championship to Atlanta.

GAME ONE

At Atlanta
October 21, 1995

The new meets the old: Atlanta's Fulton County Stadium on the right, with Olympic Stadium, the new home of the Braves, nearing completion on the left.

Eddie Murray and Marquis Grissom exchange greetings and soak up the Series atmosphere prior to the game.

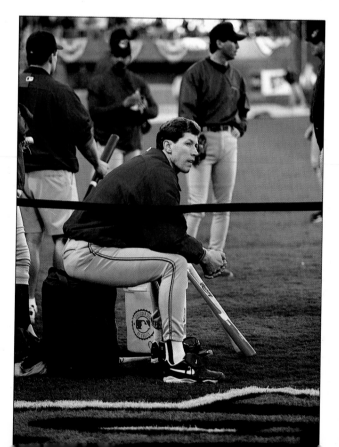

Cleveland starter Orel
Hershiser (opposite right)
collects his thoughts. Umpire
Bruce Froemming (top) rubs
up baseballs for the Series
opener.

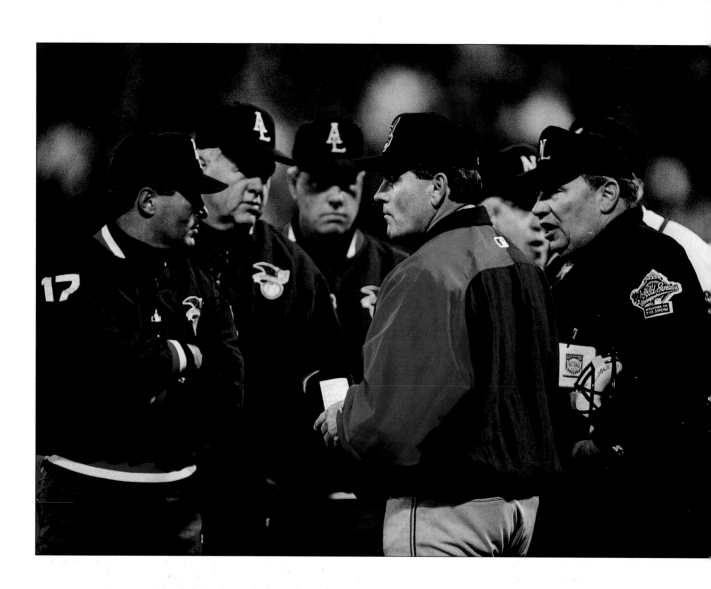

Before the game, managers and umpires go over ground rules. Cal Ripken, who during the 1995 season broke Lou Gehrig's record for consecutive games played, throws out the first pitch. Bobby Cox and Mike Hargrove (opposite) shake hands at home plate.

Atlanta's Fulton County Stadium sparkles at night. During pregame warmup, Luis Polonia and Carlos Baerga discuss the upcoming Series. Cleveland's Dave Winfield, who didn't play during the Post Season, and Tony Pena find time to play a joke on Ruben Amaro, placing a bubble gum bubble on his cap as the nation looks on.

"He (Maddux) doesn't seem dominating, then you look up at the scoreboard and you've got one hit and it's the eighth inning."
—*Jim Thome*

Atlanta ace Greg
Maddux (opposite)
picked up the win in
Game One, throwing a
complete game and
allowing only two
unearned runs. One of
those runs was courtesy
of Indians leadoff man
Kenny Lofton.

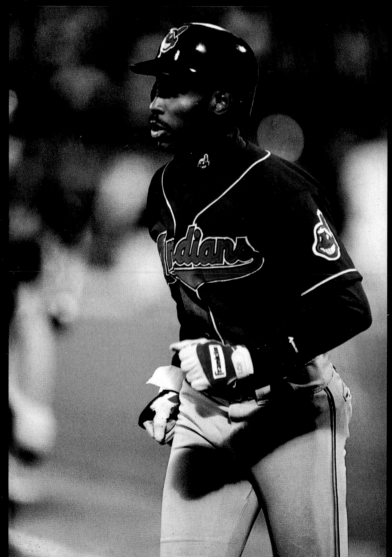

Kenny Lofton led off the game by reaching first on an error by Rafael Belliard. He then stole second and third, and scored on Carlos Baerga's ground out.

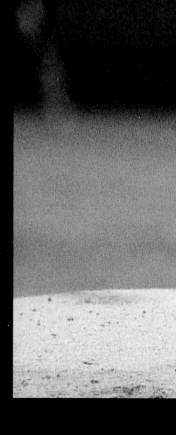

Game One starter Orel Hershiser came into the Series
with a perfect 7-0 Post Season record.

Jim Thome and Mark Lemke (opposite). Fred McGriff's homer to right-center evened the game in the second.

Two walks and a misplaced "release point" spelled the end for Hershiser in the seventh. With the bases full, Luis Polonia's roller to short was bobbled by Omar Vizquel, who still managed to get the force on Mike Devereaux at second—at least according to umpire Bruce Froemming. One run scored on the play.

"It was neither physical nor mental fatigue. I just lost my release point and I thought where the ball was going out of my hand would have been in Klesko's power area. At the time I didn't feel I was executing my pitches well enough to get him (Klesko) out."

—*Orel Hershiser*

"Orel said he was done, and when a pitcher
says he's done, he's usually done."
—*Mike Hargrove*

Braves Manager Bobby Cox takes exception with Bruce
Froemming's call at second in the seventh inning
Mark Lemke (opposite top) routinely dispatches of another Indians
hitter. Marquis Grissom (opposite bottom) was a thorn in the side of
the Indians throughout the Series

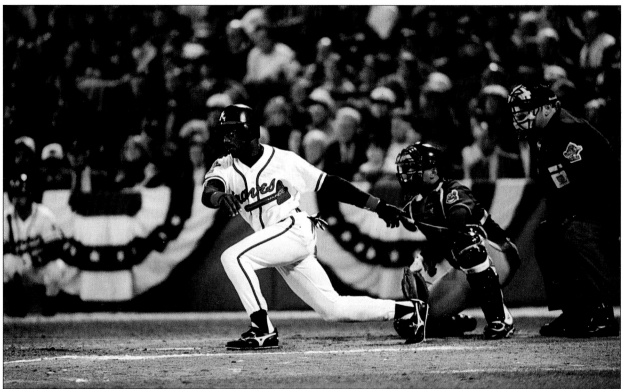

With a 3-2 win under their belts, the Braves celebrate on the field.

| Cleveland | 1 0 0 | 0 0 0 | 0 0 1 - 2 |
| Atlanta | 0 1 0 | 0 0 0 | 2 0 x - 3 |

Atlanta leads Series 1-0

GAME TWO

At Atlanta
October 22, 1995

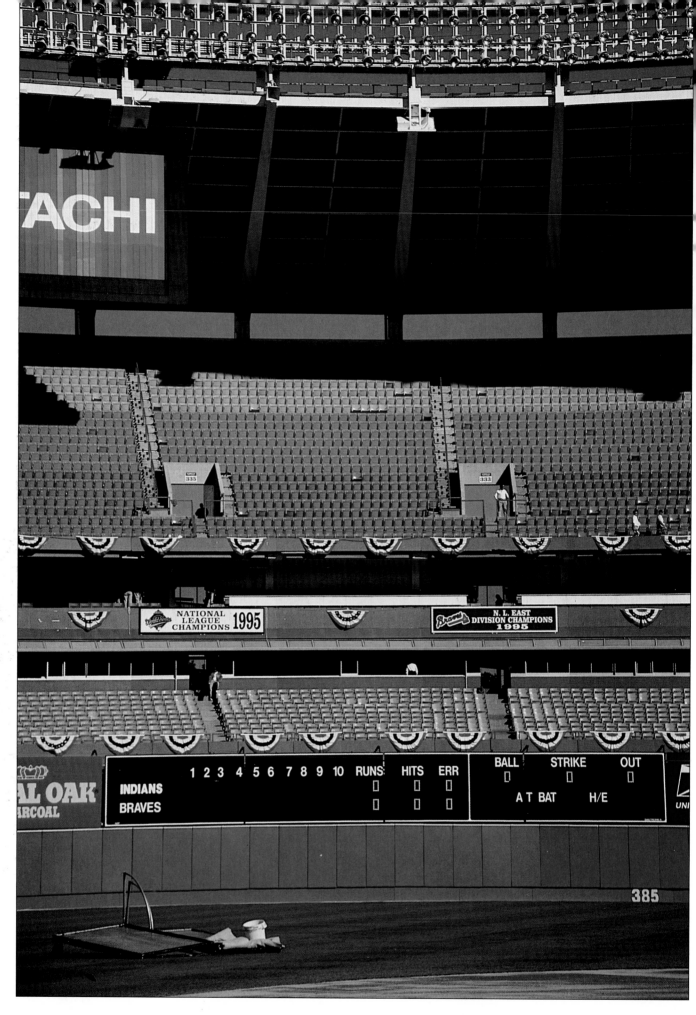

Carlos Baerga, Jim Thome, Rafael Belliard and Mark Lemke may be adversaries on the field, but prior to the game they're able to get together and enjoy the festive atmosphere that surrounds the World Series. Bobby Cox has the look of a man whose team won the first game of the Series. Cleveland starter Dennis Martinez (left) looks anything but tense as he goes through his pregame routine prior to Game Two.

Mike Hargrove and
Albert Belle focus on
Game Two (top).
Baseball's home run
king, Henry Aaron,
throws out the first
pitch.

"They're a great hitting ballclub, but at the same time, we're a pretty good pitching staff. The saying 'Good pitching beats good hitting' had to come from somewhere."
— *Tom Glavine*

Though not at his best, Tom Glavine used all his skills to give the Braves a 2-0 Series lead (left). Eddie Murray's two-run homer (bottom) in the second gave the Tribe an early lead.

Javier Lopez visits with Tom Glavine after Murray's home run. Chipper Jones makes a play, and Dennis Martinez struggles through $5\,^1/_3$ innings. Mark Lemke singled, (opposite) then scored on a Dave Justice base hit in the two-run Atlanta third.

"I thought Dennis struggled the entire game . . . I didn't say he stunk; I said he was struggling. There's a difference between the two."

—*Mike Hargrove*

Albert Belle's error on Dave Justice's leadoff single in the sixth (right) opened the door for the Braves. Marquis Grissom's single ended the evening for Dennis Martinez.

Javier Lopez drove in two runs with a monster home run in the sixth (left). Dennis Martinez worries that Game Two is slipping away. Kenny Lofton got one run back in the seventh. He singled, stole second and scored on an error by Braves left fielder Mike Devereaux.

Albert Belle vents his frustration after a strikeout (left). Manny Ramirez breaks his bat, then breaks the hearts of Tribe fans by getting picked off first in the eighth inning of Game Two.

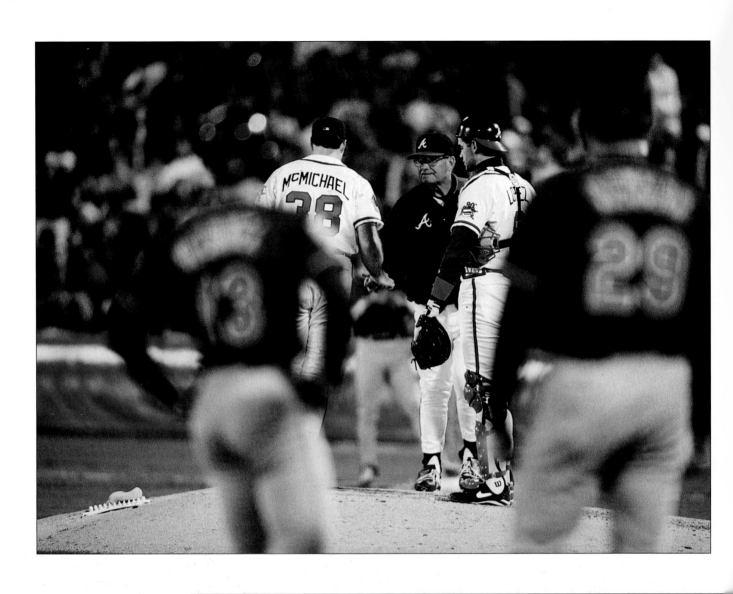

Bobby Cox, Greg McMichael and Javier Lopez meet on the mound as Cleveland's Omar Vizquel looks on from third. Mark Wohlers and Chipper Jones (opposite) celebrate the Braves' 2-0 Series lead.

"I'm looking forward to the challenge of playing in Jacobs Field. I know the fans are crazy there, but they can't be any crazier than the fans in Colorado."

—*David Justice*

Cleveland	0 2 0 0 0 0 1 0 0 - 3
Atlanta	0 0 2 0 0 2 0 0 x - 4

Atlanta leads Series 2-0

GAME THREE

At Cleveland
October 24, 1995

For the first time since 1954, Cleveland was hosting a World Series. The city and its fans made the most of the occasion, adorning buildings and themselves in Indians colors.

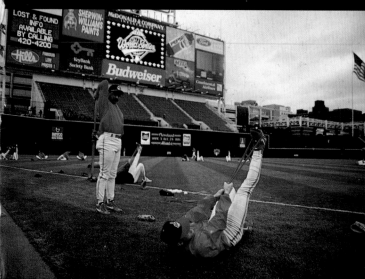

Orel Hershiser and Tom
Glavine before Game Three
(top). Ryan Klesko takes care
of some last-minute business
(opposite bottom left).

"We are a team that can win four in a row. That is our challenge. We have to do that."

—*Kenny Lofton*

Charles Nagy, who hadn't pitched in ten days, went seven innings in Game Three, giving up five runs. Chipper Jones' double in the first drove in the Braves' first run. John Smoltz (opposite) lasted only 2 1/3 innings, due in part to the hitting of Kenny Lofton, who singled in the first and doubled in the third, scoring both times.

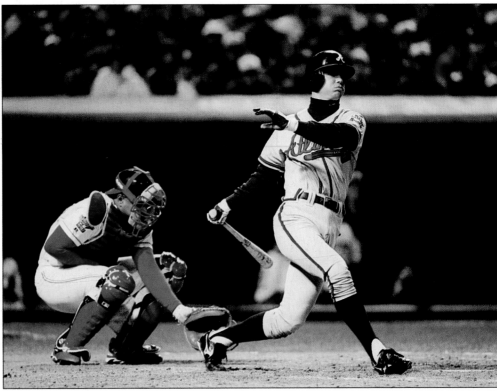

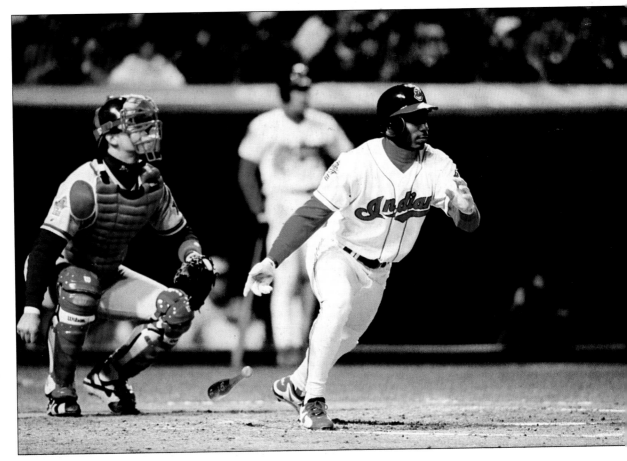

Omar Vizquel's first inning triple scored Lofton. Albert Belle's third inning single drove home Vizquel. Braves Manager Bobby Cox removes John Smoltz (opposite). Everyone's in motion as Manny Ramirez grounds into a double play in the third.

"We had a little bit of a pep talk in the clubhouse, I think Kenny initiated it, just to talk about how we needed to go out there, relax and let our talent take over."
—Sandy Alomar

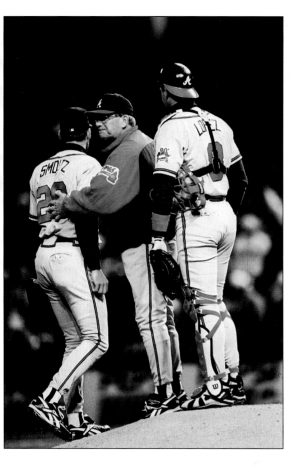

"I honestly didn't think I made that many bad pitches. They just hit them where our fielders weren't."
—*John Smoltz*

Fred McGriff (opposite) and Ryan Klesko take Charles Nagy deep in the sixth and seventh innings, respectively. Carlos Baerga shows perfect form as he waits for the ball.

"Kenny Lofton's speed can distort a game."
—*Mike Hargrove*

Carlos Baerga's infield single (opposite) in the seventh scores Kenny Lofton, who had walked, moved to second on a ground out, then stole third. Paul Assenmacher's outing (left) lasted only 1/3 of an inning. Manny Ramirez walked and scored in the eighth to tie the game at 6.

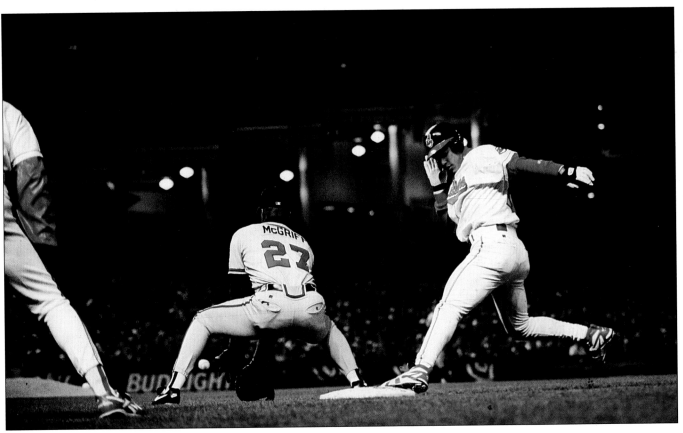

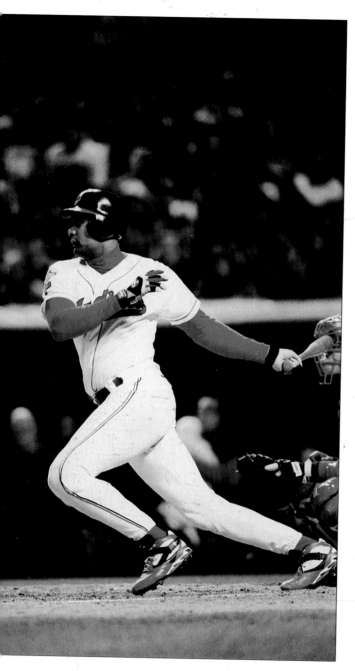

Sandy Alomar's eighth inning double sent the game to extra innings. Jose Mesa threw three sparkling innings for the win, but he got some nice defensive help, including an 11th inning double play (right). Eddie Murray singled in pinch runner Alvaro Espinoza in the 11th to give Cleveland the win.

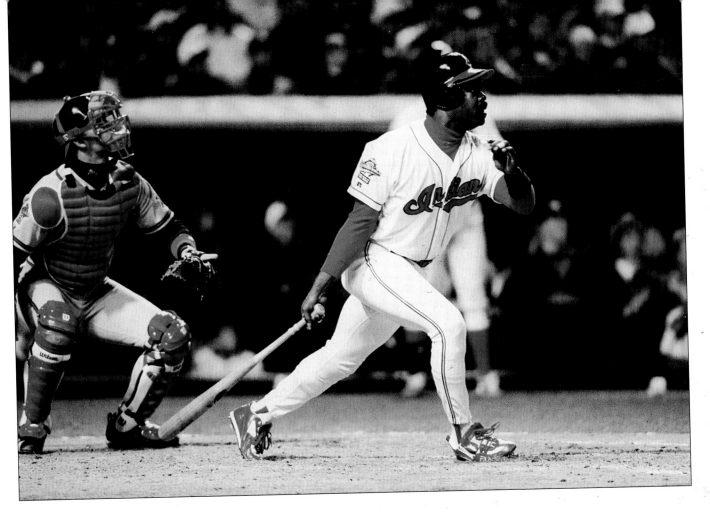

Atlanta	100 001 130 00 - 6
Cleveland	202 000 110 01 - 7

Atlanta leads Series 2-1

GAME FOUR

At Cleveland
October 25, 1995

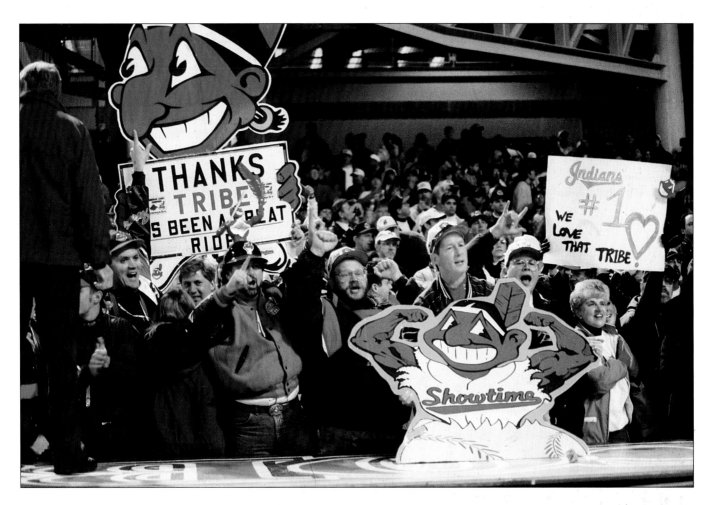

"Do we have to validate our season? No. Do we want to win? You bet. There were 28 teams, and now there are two. That speaks for itself. We didn't come here to lose."

—*Cleveland Manager Mike Hargrove*

Tom Glavine (left) and a writer discuss the Series.

The Series takes on a completely different look when viewed from high above in the blimp. Inside the blimp (right) the crew monitors the action below.

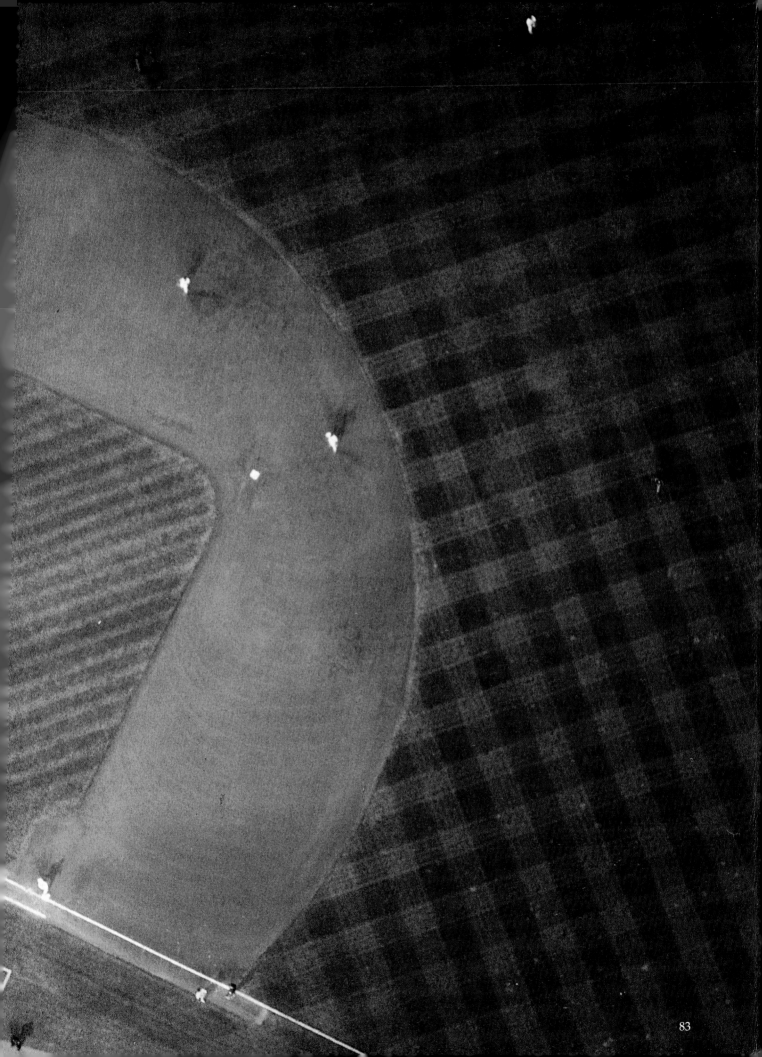

"I've got faith in my guys. I've been trying to tell people there's a hell of a lot more to this pitching staff than Greg Maddux."

—*Bobby Cox*

Ken Hill (top) worked 6 1/3 innings and took the loss. Steve Avery (opposite) rewarded Manager Bobby Cox's faith in him, going 6 innings for the win. Atlanta leadoff hitter Marquis Grissom was a thorn in the side of the Indians during Game Four.

Javier Lopez doubles in the fourth, then fires to second in the fifth in an attempt to pick-off Alvaro Espinoza. Ryan Klesko's sixth inning home run (opposite) gave Atlanta a 1-0 lead.

Albert Belle (opposite) answered Klesko with a solo shot of his own in the bottom of the sixth. Luis Polonia's double drove in a run during Atlanta's three-run seventh, while Jim Thome's double in the same inning amounted to nothing for the Tribe.

"It's safe to say I won't be
sleeping much tonight."
—*Chipper Jones*

Marquis Grissom (opposite) went 3 for
4 in Game Four. Julian Tavarez works
in the eighth for Cleveland, and Rafael
Belliard lays down a sacrifice bunt in
the eighth.

Paul Sorrento's double (top, with Chipper Jones) followed the Manny Ramirez homer, and put an end to Mark Wohlers' night.

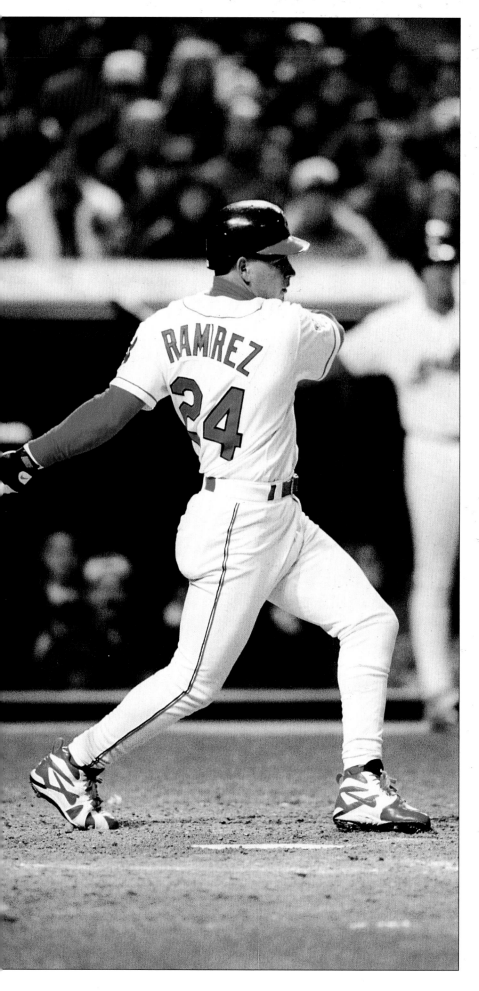

Pedro Borbon picked up the save,
giving Atlanta a 3-1 advantage.

Atlanta	000	001	301-5
Cleveland	000	001	001-2

Atlanta leads Series 3-1

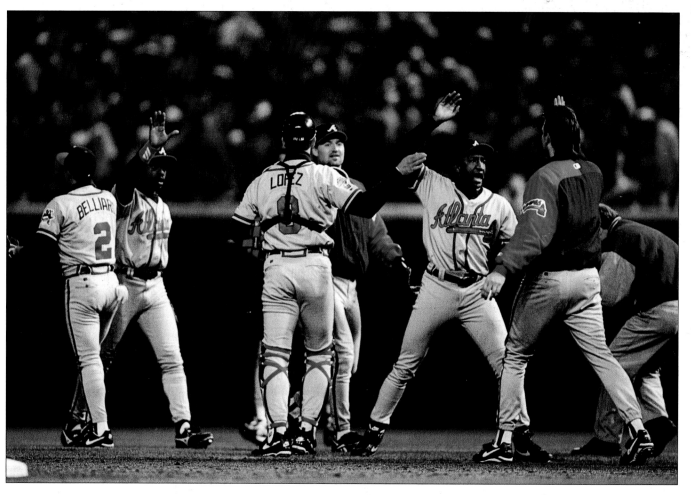

GAME FIVE

At Cleveland
October 26, 1995

"The fans don't get mad at you if you don't win the World Series the first time you go. You have a big parade, they tell you that you did okay. The next year, if you go and don't win, they boo."

—*Bobby Cox*

Orel Hershiser (opposite) returned to his "Bulldog" form in Game Five. Chipper Jones had a double in the first, but was stranded when Fred McGriff struck out.

"We beat their best, now it's time to take care of
everybody else."
— *Kenny Lofton*

Greg Maddux (opposite) faced Orel Hershiser in a Game One rematch. Omar Vizquel was on second when Albert Belle homered to right in the second, giving Cleveland a 2-0 lead.

Greg Maddux brushed back Eddie Murray after the Belle home run, clearing the benches. Jim Thome (opposite) went 2 for 4 in Game Five, driving in two runs.

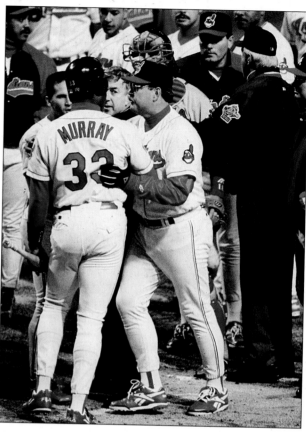

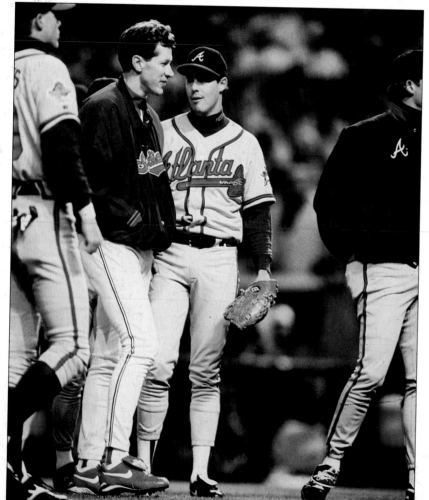

During the bench-clearing incident, Orel Hershiser and Greg Maddux found themselves together on the mound . . . a unusual scene.

"We didn't come to fight, but that definitely woke us up. We had to let people know we won't be intimidated."

—Sandy Alomar

Luis Polonia and Charlie O'Brien of Atlanta figured into the action in Game Five. Polonia homered in the fourth, while O'Brien's sacrifice set the table in the fifth.

"I don't let my on-field emotions affect my off-field and everyday life. I build a crescendo and then can release it in the three hours during the game. I can change the emotions when I take off the uniform. I think my family can appreciate that."

—Orel Hershiser

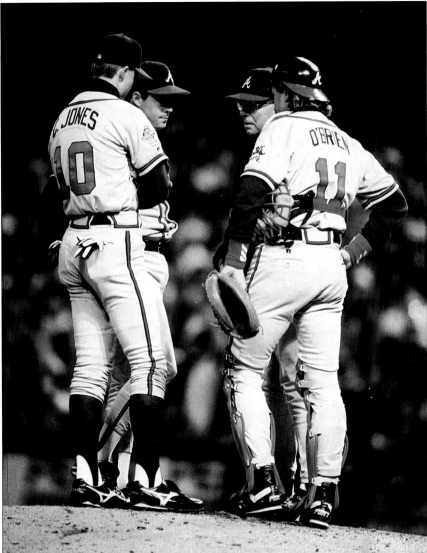

Sandy Alomar doubles in the fifth. Greg Maddux lasted seven innings for the Braves, but, admittedly, didn't have his best stuff working. He took the loss.

Jose Mesa (left) earned the save despite giving up a two-run shot in the ninth. Brad Clontz (top) relieved Greg Maddux in the eighth, then gave up a homer to Jim Thome (opposite) which turned out to be the difference in the game.

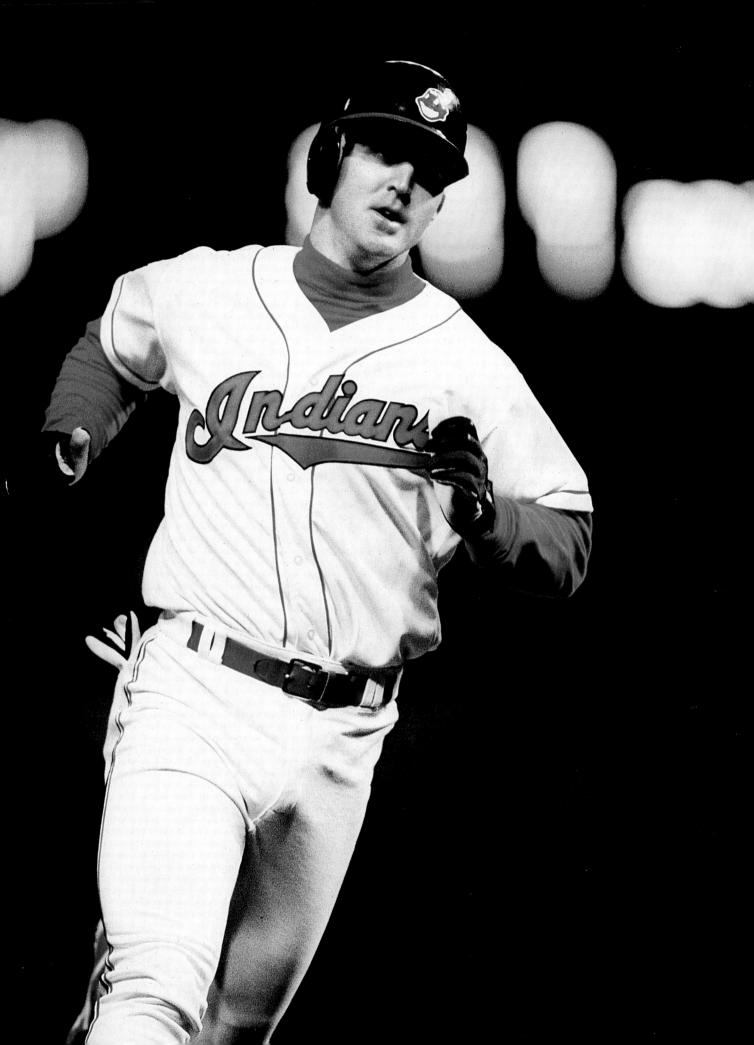

Mike Mordecai (opposite top) singled in the eighth, then was doubled-up when Hershiser stabbed a line drive up the middle and threw to first. Ryan Klesko's ninth inning home run (opposite bottom) brought the Braves back to within one, but that's where the game ended.

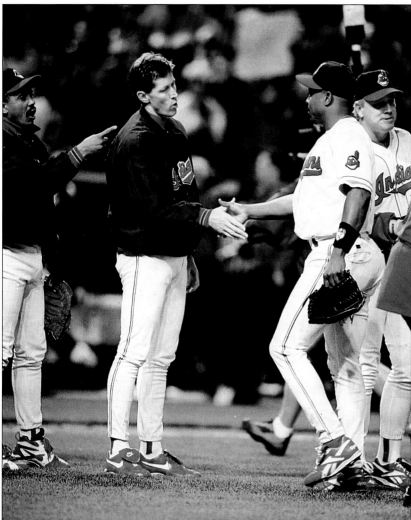

Atlanta	000	110	002 - 4
Cleveland	200	002	01 x - 5

Atlanta leads Series 3-2

GAME SIX

At Atlanta
October 28, 1995

"You don't fret about people second guessing you, even though you pick up the paper every day to see you're pitching the wrong guy."
— *Bobby Cox*

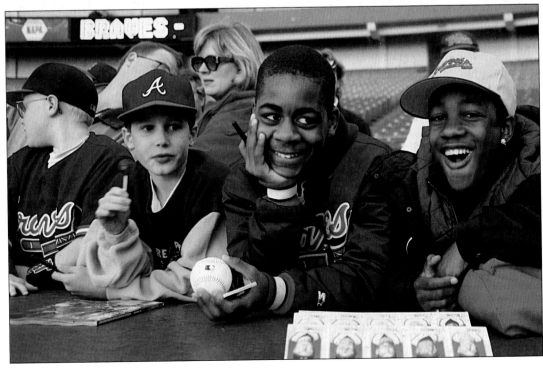

Series MVP Tom Glavine (opposite) threw eight innings of shutout ball for his second win of the Series. Former President Jimmy Carter and wife Rosalynn enjoy the action with Bill Murray (right).

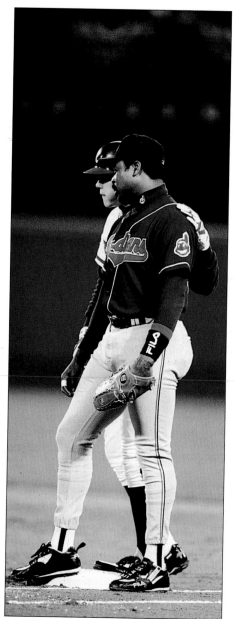

120

Dennis Martinez (opposite) didn't make it out of the fifth inning, but allowed no runs. Eddie Murray and Chipper Jones discuss the action. Mark Lemke (left) tags out Albert Belle. Carlos Baerga (bottom) is upended while turning two.

Dennis Martinez and Tony Pena discuss their options (top). Jim Poole (opposite top left) gave up the game's only run. Tony Pena (opposite top right) collected the Tribe's lone hit.

"Their starting pitching is deeper than we've seen. We didn't see their bullpen much."
—*Mike Hargrove*

With Tom Glavine shutting down Cleveland, the sixth inning home run by David Justice off Jim Poole was all the scoring the Braves needed to wrap up their first championship.

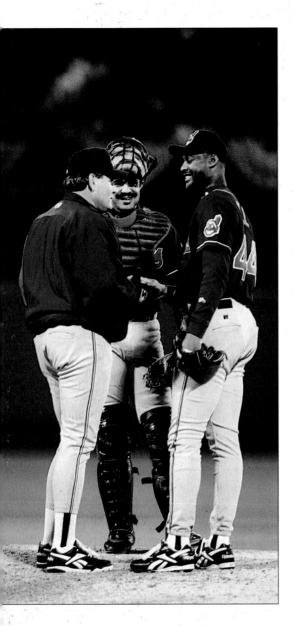

Ken Hill faced one hitter. Eddie Murray (opposite top) searches for a hit. Javier Lopez (opposite bottom) thrusts his arms skyward to celebrate his apparent eighth inning home run . . . unfortunately, the ball stayed in the park.

"It was really difficult. I really wanted to be on the field and jump around with the guys at the end of the game."
—*Tom Glavine*

Orel Hershiser (opposite) ponders what might have been. Paul Assenmacher hopes a new baseball will turn things around, but the Tribe's fate is spelled out in a fan's sign.

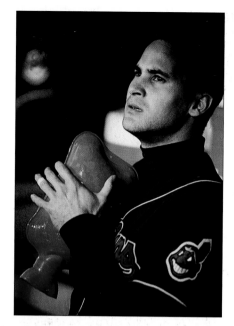

Reflection and sadness are etched on the faces of the
Indians as the celebration begins for the Braves.

Cleveland	000 000 000 - 0
Atlanta	000 001 00x - 1

Atlanta wins Series 4-2

131

Mark Wohlers and Javier Lopez
embrace after the final out
(opposite), then are swarmed by
the rest of the Braves.

David Justice and Greg Maddux enjoy the moment (opposite). Tony Pena, equipment in tow, leaves a quiet Cleveland dugout.

"I've seen Tommy throw a lot of great games, but given the circumstances and the pressure on us all, he was about as good as I've ever seen him. What he did was put a stamp on five years of great pitching."
—Leo Mazzone

The Agony of Defeat

Greg Maddux, Charlie O'Brien and Jane Fonda
enjoy the Braves' first championship in
Atlanta.   Answering post game questions are,
clockwise, Bobby Cox, Tom Glavine, Omar
Vizquel, Mike Hargrove and Dennis Martinez.

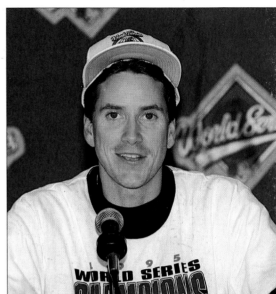

"We played well, they played well—we have nothing to be ashamed of."
—Jim Thome

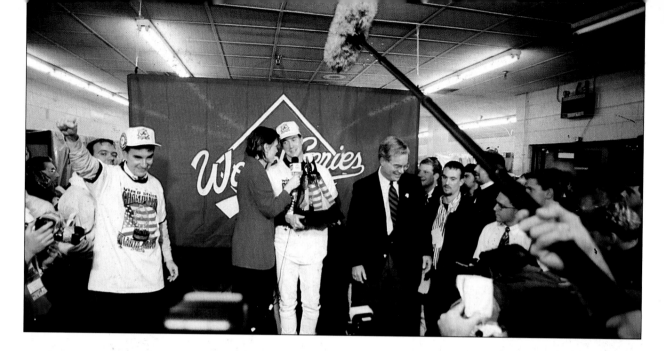

"We're going to have a parade-o-grand-ay.
At last, at last!"
        —*Ted Turner*

Tom Glavine (opposite) receives his MVP Trophy.
Ted Turner (above) displays the World Series Trophy
and Fred McGriff displays a winner's smile.

THE WORLD SERIES IN NUMBERS

GAME ONE

Cleveland	ab	r	h	bi
Lofton cf	4	2	1	0
Vizquel ss	4	0	0	0
Baerga 2b	4	0	0	1
Belle lf	3	0	0	0
Murray 1b	3	0	0	0
Tavarez p	0	0	0	0
Embree p	0	0	0	0
Thome 3b	3	0	1	0
Ramirez rf	3	0	0	0
Alomar c	3	0	0	0
Hershiser p	2	0	0	0
Assenmacher p	0	0	0	0
Sorrento 1b	1	0	0	0
Totals	30	2	2	1

Atlanta	ab	r	h	bi
Grissom cf	4	0	1	0
Lemke 2b	3	0	1	0
Jones 3b	4	0	0	0
McGriff 1b	3	2	1	1
Justice rf	1	1	0	0
Klesko lf	2	0	0	0
Devereaux ph-lf	0	0	0	0
O'Brien c	2	0	0	0
Polonia ph	1	0	0	1
Lopez c	0	0	0	0
Belliard ss	2	0	0	1
Maddux p	3	0	0	0
Totals	25	3	3	3

Cleveland	1 0 0	0 0 0	0 0 1	— 2
Atlanta	0 1 0	0 0 0	2 0 x	— 3

E-McGriff (1), Belliard (1). LOB-Cleveland 1, Atlanta 4. HR-McGriff (1). RBIs-Baerga (1), McGriff (1), Polonia (1), Belliard (1). SB-Lofton 2 (2). S-Belliard. DP-Cleveland 1 (Vizquel and Baerga).

Cleveland	IP	H	R	ER	BB	SO
Hershiser L (0-1)	6	3	3	3	3	7
Assenmacher	0	0	0	0	1	0
Tavarez	1.1	0	0	0	1	0
Embree	0.2	0	0	0	0	2

Atlanta	IP	H	R	ER	BB	SO
Maddux W (1-0)	9	2	2	0	0	4

Hershiser pitched to 2 batters in the 7th, Assenmacher pitched to 1 batter in the 7th.
T-2:37. A-51,876 (52,710). Umpires-HP, Wendelstedt; 1B, McKean; 2B, Froemming; 3B, Hirschbeck; LF, Pulli; RF, Brinkman.

GAME TWO

Cleveland	ab	r	h	bi
Lofton cf	5	1	1	0
Vizquel ss	4	0	1	0
Baerga 2b	4	0	0	0
Belle lf	3	1	1	0
Murray 1b	3	1	1	2
Ramirez rf	4	0	2	0
Thome 3b	3	0	0	0
TPena c	3	0	0	0
Sorrento ph	1	0	0	0
Alomar c	0	0	0	0
Martinez p	2	0	0	0
Embree p	0	0	0	0
Kirby ph	1	0	0	0
Poole p	0	0	0	0
Tavarez p	0	0	0	0
Amaro ph	1	0	0	0
Totals	34	3	6	2

Atlanta	ab	r	h	bi
Grissom cf	3	1	1	0
Lemke 2b	3	1	1	0
Jones 3b	3	0	2	1
McGriff 1b	4	0	0	0
Justice rf	3	1	2	1
Wohlers p	0	0	0	0
Klesko lf	3	0	0	0
Devereaux lf-rf	1	0	0	0
Lopez c	3	1	1	2
Belliard ss	4	0	0	0
Glavine p	1	0	0	0
Smith ph	1	0	1	0
McMichael p	0	0	0	0
APena p	0	0	0	0
Polonia lf	0	0	0	0
Totals	29	4	8	4

Cleveland	0 2 0	0 0 0	1 0 0	— 3
Atlanta	0 0 2	0 0 2	0 0 x	— 4

E-Belle (1), Martinez (1), Jones (1), Devereaux (1). LOB-Cleveland 9, Atlanta 7. 2B-Jones (1). HR-Lopez (1), Murray (1). RBIs-Murray 2 (2), Jones (1), Justice (1), Lopez 2 (2). SB-Lofton 2 (4), Vizquel (1). SF-Jones. DP-Cleveland 2 (Baerga, Vizquel and Murray), (Vizquel, Baerga and Murray).

Cleveland	IP	H	R	ER	BB	SO
Martinez L (0-1)	5.2	8	4	4	3	3
Embree	.1	0	0	0	0	0
Poole	1	0	0	0	0	0
Tavarez	1	0	0	0	0	0

Atlanta	IP	H	R	ER	BB	SO
Glavine W (1-0)	6	3	2	2	3	3
McMichael	.2	1	1	0	1	1
APena	1	1	0	0	1	0
Wohlers S (1)	1.1	1	0	0	0	1

HBP-by Martinez (Grissom), by Tavarez (Lopez). WP-Glavine, McMichael. T-3:17. A-51,877 (52,710). Umpires-HP, McKean; 1B, Froemming; 2B, Hirschbeck; 3B, Pulli; LF, Brinkman; RF, Wendelstedt.

GAME THREE

Atlanta	ab	r	h	bi
Grissom cf	6	1	2	0
Polonia lf	4	1	1	1
Jones 3b	3	2	1	0
McGriff 1b	5	1	3	2
Justice rf	5	0	0	1
Klesko dh	3	1	2	1
Devereaux ph-dh	2	0	1	1
Lopez c	5	0	0	0
Lemke 2b	5	0	2	0
Belliard ss	2	0	0	0
Smith ph	1	0	0	0
Mordecai ss	1	0	0	0
Totals	42	6	12	6

Cleveland	ab	r	h	bi
Lofton cf	3	3	3	0
Vizquel ss	6	2	2	1
Baerga 2b	6	0	3	3
Espinoza pr	0	1	0	0
Belle lf	4	0	1	1
Murray dh	6	0	1	1
Thome 3b	4	0	0	0
Ramirez rf	2	1	0	0
Sorrento 1b	4	0	1	0
Kirby pr	0	0	0	0
Perry 1b	1	0	0	0
Alomar c	5	0	1	1
Totals	41	7	12	7

Atlanta	1 0 0	0 0 1	1 3 0	0 0	— 6
Cleveland	2 0 2	0 0 0	1 1 0	0 1	— 7

No outs when winning run scored.
E-Belliard (2), Baerga (1), Sorrento (1). LOB-Atlanta 7, Cleveland 13. 2B-Grissom (1), Jones (2), Lofton (1), Baerga (1), Alomar (1). 3B-Vizquel (1). HR-McGriff (2), Klesko (1). RBIs-McGriff 2 (3), Klesko (1), Polonia (2), Justice (2), Devereaux (1), Vizquel (1), Baerga 3 (4), Belle (1), Alomar (1), Murray (3). CS-Grissom (1), Lofton (1). S-Mordecai. DP-Atlanta 1 (Lemke and McGriff); Cleveland 2 (Baerga, Vizquel and Sorrento), (Baerga, Vizquel and Perry).

Atlanta	IP	H	R	ER	BB	SO
Smoltz	2.1	6	4	4	2	4
Clontz	2.1	1	0	0	0	1
Mercker	2	1	1	1	2	2
McMichael	.2	1	1	1	1	1
Wohlers	2.2	1	0	0	3	2
APena L (0-1)	0	2	1	1	1	0

Cleveland	IP	H	R	ER	BB	SO
Nagy	7	8	5	5	1	4
Assenmacher	.1	0	1	1	10	0
Tavarez	.2	1	0	0	0	0
Mesa W (1-0)	3	3	0	0	1	3

Nagy pitched to 2 batters in the 8th, APena pitched to 3 batters in the 11th.
T-4:09. A-43,584 (42,865). Umpires-HP, Froemming; 1B, Hirschbeck; 2B, Pulli; 3B, Brinkman; LF, Wendelstedt; RF, McKean.

CLEVELAND INDIANS

PLAYER	G	AB	R	H	Batting 2B	3B	HR	RBI	BB	SO	AVG.
Espinoza	2	2	1	1	0	0	0	0	0	0	.500
Belle	6	17	4	4	0	0	2	4	7	5	.235
Ramirez	6	18	2	4	0	0	1	2	4	5	.222
Thome	6	19	1	4	1	0	1	2	2	5	.211
Lofton	6	25	6	5	1	0	0	0	3	1	.200
Alomar	5	15	0	3	2	0	0	1	0	2	.200
Baerga	6	26	1	5	2	0	0	4	1	1	.192
Sorrento	5	11	0	2	1	0	0	0	0	4	.182
Vizquel	6	23	3	4	0	1	0	1	3	5	.174
TPena	2	6	0	1	0	0	0	0	0	0	.167
Murray	6	19	1	2	0	0	1	3	5	4	.105
Perry	3	5	0	0	0	0	0	0	0	2	.000
Martinez	2	3	0	0	0	0	0	0	0	1	.000
Amaro	2	2	0	0	0	0	0	0	0	1	.000
Hershiser	2	2	0	0	0	0	0	0	0	0	.000
Kirby	3	1	0	0	0	0	0	0	0	1	.000
Poole	2	1	0	0	0	0	0	0	0	0	.000
TOTALS	6	195	19	35	7	1	5	17	25	37	.179

PITCHER	G	IP	H	R	Pitching BB	SO	HB	W	L	ERA
Tavarez	5	4.1	3	0	2	1	1	0	0	0.00
Hershiser	2	14	8	5	4	13	0	1	1	2.57
Embree	4	3.1	2	1	2	2	0	0	0	2.70
Martinez	2	10.1	12	4	8	5	1	0	1	3.48
Poole	2	2.1	1	1	0	1	0	0	1	3.86
Hill	2	6.1	7	3	4	1	0	0	1	4.26
Mesa	2	4	5	2	1	4	0	1	0	4.50
Nagy	1	7	8	5	1	4	0	0	0	6.43
Asnmchr	4	1.1	1	2	3	3	0	0	0	6.75
TOTALS	6	53	47	23	25	34	2	2	4	3.57

Complete games—None. Saves—Mesa 1.

THE WORLD SERIES IN NUMBERS

GAME FOUR

Atlanta	ab	r	h	bi
Grissom cf	4	1	3	0
Polonia lf	4	1	2	1
Devereaux lf	0	0	0	0
Jones 3b	4	1	0	0
McGriff 1b	3	1	1	0
Justice rf	5	0	1	2
Klesko dh	3	1	1	1
Mordecai ph-dh	1	0	0	0
Lopez c	5	0	2	1
Lemke 2b	5	0	1	0
Belliard ss	3	0	0	0
Totals	37	5	11	5

Cleveland	ab	r	h	bi
Lofton cf	5	0	0	0
Vizquel ss	3	0	0	0
Baerga 2b	4	0	1	0
Belle lf	3	1	1	1
Murray dh	2	0	0	0
Ramirez rf	3	1	1	1
Perry 1b	3	0	0	0
Sorrento ph	1	0	1	0
Espinoza 3b	2	0	1	0
Thome ph-3b	2	0	1	0
Alomar c	4	0	0	0
Totals	32	2	6	2

Atlanta	000 001 301	—	5
Cleveland	000 001 001	—	2

E-Lemke (1). LOB-Atlanta 12, Cleveland 8. 2B-Polonia (1), McGriff (1), Lopez 2(2), Sorrento (1), Thome (1). HR-Belle (1), Ramirez (1), Klesko 2(2). RBIs-Polonia (3), Justice 2(4), Klesko (2), Lopez (3), Belle (2), Ramirez (1). SB-Grissom 2(2). CS-Espinoza (1). S-Belliard. DP-Atlanta 1 (Jones, Lemke and McGriff).

Atlanta	IP	H	R	ER	BB	SO
Avery W (1-0)	6	3	1	1	5	3
McMichael	2	1	0	0	0	0
Wohlers	0	2	1	1	0	0
Borbon S (1)	1	0	0	0	0	2

Cleveland	IP	H	R	ER	BB	SO
Hill L (0-1)	6.1	6	3	3	4	1
Assenmacher	.2	1	1	0	1	2
Tavarez	.2	2	0	0	1	1
Embree	1.1	2	1	1	0	0

Wohlers pitched to 2 batters in the 9th.
PB-Alomar. Balk-Avery. T-3:14. A-43,578 (42,865). Umpires-HP, Hirschbeck; 1B, Pulli; 2B, Brinkman; 3B, Wendelstedt; LF, McKean; RF, Froemming.

GAME FIVE

Atlanta	ab	r	h	bi
Grissom cf	4	0	1	1
Polonia lf	4	1	1	1
Jones 3b	4	0	1	0
McGriff 1b	4	1	1	0
Justice rf	4	0	0	0
Klesko dh	4	2	2	2
Lemke 2b	4	0	0	0
O'Brien c	1	0	0	0
Lopez ph-c	1	0	0	0
Belliard ss	1	0	0	0
Smith ph	0	0	0	0
Mordecai ss	1	0	1	0
Totals	32	4	7	4

Cleveland	ab	r	h	bi
Lofton cf	4	0	0	0
Vizquel ss	3	1	1	0
Baerga 2b	4	1	1	0
Belle lf	3	2	1	2
Murray dh	3	0	0	0
Thome 3b	4	1	2	2
Ramirez rf	3	0	1	1
Perry 1b	1	0	0	0
Sorrento 1b	3	0	0	0
Kirby rf	0	0	0	0
Alomar c	3	0	2	0
Totals	31	5	8	5

Atlanta	000 110 002	—	4
Cleveland	200 002 01x	—	5

E-Hershiser (1). LOB-Atlanta 3, Cleveland 5. 2B-Jones (3), McGriff (2), Baerga (2), Alomar (2). HR-Belle (2); Thome (1); Polonia (1); Klesko (3). RBIs-Grissom (1), Polonia (4), Klesko 2 (4), Belle 2(4), Thome 2 (2), Ramirez (2). S-O'Brien. DP-Cleveland 2 (Vizquel, Baerga and Sorrento), (Hershiser and Perry).

Atlanta	IP	H	R	ER	BB	SO
Maddux L (1-1)	7	7	4	4	3	4
Clontz	1	1	1	1	0	1

Cleveland	IP	H	R	ER	BB	SO
Hershiser W (1-1)	8	5	2	1	1	6
Mesa S (1)	1	2	2	2	0	1

IBB-by Maddux (Belle) 1, by Hershiser (Smith) 1. T-2:33. A-43,595 (42,865). Umpires-HP, Pulli; 1B, Brinkman; 2B, Wendelstedt; 3B, McKean; LF, Froemming; RF, Hirschbeck.

GAME SIX

Cleveland	ab	r	h	bi
Lofton cf	4	0	0	0
Vizquel ss	3	0	0	0
Sorrento ph	1	0	0	0
Baerga 2b	4	0	0	0
Belle lf	1	0	0	0
Murray 1b	2	0	0	0
Ramirez rf	3	0	0	0
Embree p	0	0	0	0
Tavarez p	0	0	0	0
Thome 3b	3	0	0	0
TPena c	3	0	1	0
Martinez p	1	0	0	0
Poole p	1	0	0	0
Hill p	0	0	0	0
Amaro rf	1	0	0	0
Totals	27	0	1	0

Atlanta	ab	r	h	bi
Grissom cf	4	0	1	0
Lemke 2b	2	0	1	0
Jones 3b	3	0	2	0
McGriff 1b	4	0	0	0
Justice rf	2	1	2	1
Klesko lf	1	0	0	0
Devereaux lf	1	0	0	0
Lopez c	3	0	0	0
Belliard ss	4	0	0	0
Glavine p	3	0	0	0
Polonia ph	1	0	0	0
Wohlers p	0	0	0	0
Totals	28	1	6	1

Cleveland	000 000 000	—	0
Atlanta	000 001 00x	—	1

E-Thome (1). LOB-Cleveland 3, Atlanta 11. 2B-Justice (1). HR-Justice (1). RBIs-Justice (5). SB-Lofton (6), Grissom (3). CS-Belle (1), Lemke (1). S-Lemke. DP-Cleveland 1 (Martinez, Vizquel, Baerga and Murray).

Cleveland	IP	H	R	ER	BB	SO
Martinez	4.2	4	0	0	5	2
Poole L (0-1)	1.1	1	1	1	0	1
Hill	0	1	0	0	0	0
Embree	1	0	0	0	2	0
Tavarez	.2	0	0	0	0	0
Assenmacher	.1	0	0	0	0	1

Atlanta	IP	H	R	ER	BB	SO
Glavine W (2-0)	8	1	0	0	3	8
Wohlers S (2)	1	0	0	0	0	0

Hill pitched to 1 batter in the 7th.
T-3:02. A-51,875 (52,710). Umpires-HP, Brinkman; 1B, Wendelstedt; 2B, McKean; 3B, Froemming; LF, Hirschbeck; RF, Pulli.

ATLANTA BRAVES

Batting

PLAYER	G	AB	R	H	2B	3B	HR	RBI	BB	SO	AVG.
Smith	3	2	0	1	0	0	0	0	1	0	.500
Grissom	6	25	3	9	1	0	0	1	1	3	.360
Mordecai	3	3	0	1	0	0	0	0	0	1	.333
Klesko	6	16	4	5	0	0	3	4	3	4	.313
Jones	6	21	3	6	3	0	0	1	4	5	.286
Polonia	6	14	3	4	1	0	1	4	1	3	.286
Lemke	6	22	1	6	0	0	0	0	3	2	.273
McGriff	6	23	5	6	2	0	2	3	3	5	.261
Justice	6	20	3	5	1	0	1	5	5	1	.250
Devereaux	5	4	0	1	0	0	0	1	2	1	.250
Lopez	6	17	1	3	2	0	1	3	1	1	.176
Belliard	6	16	0	0	0	0	0	1	0	4	.000
Glavine	2	4	0	0	0	0	0	0	1	2	.000
O'Brien	2	3	0	0	0	0	0	0	0	1	.000
Maddux	2	3	0	0	0	0	0	0	0	1	.000
TOTALS	6	193	23	47	10	0	8	23	25	34	.244

Pitching

PITCHER	G	IP	H	R	BB	SO	HB	W	L	ERA
Borbon	1	1	0	0	0	2	0	0	0	0.00
Glavine	2	14	4	2	6	11	0	2	0	1.29
Avery	1	6	3	1	5	3	0	1	0	1.50
Wohlers	4	5	4	1	3	3	0	0	0	1.80
Maddux	2	16	9	6	3	8	0	1	1	2.25
Clontz	2	3.1	2	1	0	2	0	0	0	2.70
McMichael	3	3.1	3	2	2	2	0	0	0	2.70
Merker	1	2	1	1	2	2	0	0	0	4.50
APena	2	1	3	1	2	0	0	0	1	9.00
Smoltz	1	2.1	6	4	2	4	0	0	0	15.43
TOTALS	6	54	35	19	25	37	0	4	2	2.67

Complete games—Maddux 1.
Saves—Borbon 1, Wohlers 2.

The publisher wishes to thank the following companies for their support:

A KeyCorp Bank

BlueCross BlueShield of Ohio

Fuji Film

JC Penney

Just Film

The New Lab

SPORTSCHANNEL

WUAB-TV

The Ashtabula Star Beacon

Canton Repository

Columbus Ledger-Enquirer

Elyria Chronicle-Telegram

The Greenville News

Marietta Daily Journal

The Meadville Tribune

Medina County Gazette

The New Castle News

The News-Record

The Salem News

The Tribune Chronicle

A SERIES FOR THE FANS
is a production of Woodford Publishing, Inc.

PUBLISHER AND CREATIVE DIRECTOR
Laurence J. Hyman

EDITOR
Rob Kelly

ASSISTANT EDITOR
Heather Torain

ART DIRECTOR
Jim Santore

MARKETING ASSISTANTS
Paul Durham
Debbie Fong

MARKETING DIRECTOR
David Lilienstein

COMPTROLLER
Christine Abshere

ADVERTISING DIRECTOR
Tony Khing

PHOTOGRAPHERS
Tom DiPace
Stephen Green
Beth Hansen
Laurence J. Hyman
David Lilienstein
Rich Pilling
Michael Zagaris

PHOTOGRAPHY EDITOR
Dennis Desprois

WRITERS
Ron Fimrite
Rob Kelly

WOODFORD PRESS
660 Market Street, San Francisco, CA 94104

Produced in partnership with and licensed by
MAJOR LEAGUE BASEBALL PROPERTIES, INC.

VICE PRESIDENT OF PUBLISHING
Michael Bernstein

MANAGER, PUBLISHING
Dana Nicole Williams

ADMINISTRATOR, PUBLISHING
Denise Lawlor

Photo Credits

Tom DiPace: 121 (B), 124 (T), 140 (B)

Stephen Green: 9 (T), 10, 11 (T & B), 13 (T), 19 (T), 20 (BR), 22 (T), 23, 24 (B), 27 (T), 28, 31 (BL), 36, 37 (BR), 41 (TL), 43 (B), 44 (B), 46 (T), 47 (T & BR), 56 (BL), 57 (T), 59 (BL), 60-61, 70 (B), 73 (BL), 77 (BR), 79 (B), 84 (T), 85, 89 (B), 90, 95, 103, 104 (TL), 106 (B), 110 (TL & TR), 111, 114 (B), 115 (B), 117 (C), 125 (BL & BR), 127, 128, 130 (TL, C, BL, & BR), 131 (TL & TR) 133 (BR), 134 (B), 135, 136, 137 (TR), 138 (T & BR)

Beth Hansen: 6, 14-15, 16, 17, 20 (T), 31 (BR), 38-39, 41 (BR), 54, 55, 57 (BL & BR), 58 (B), 59 (BR), 62, 63, 67 (TR), 73 (BR), 78 (BL & BR), 79 (TR) 86 (BL), 112-113, 114 (T), 115 (TL & TR), 116, 117 (T), 120 (TR), 129 (B), 131 (BR), 134 (TL), 141 (B), Back Cover (TR & BR)

Laurence J. Hyman: 40, 137 (BL), 138 (BL)

David Lilienstein: 7, 13 (B), 18, 19 (B), 25, 37 (T), 50 (B), 52-53, 56 (T), 59 (T), 67 (B), 74-75, 77 (T), 78 (T), 80, 81, 82-83, 96-97, 117 (B), 131 (BL), 133 (T), 139 (TL, TR & BL), Back Cover (TC & BCR)

Rich Pilling: 2-3, 11 (C), 12 (T), 20 (BL), 21 (T), 26, 29, 30 (T), 32 (T), 33 (B), 34, 35 (T), 37 (BL), 42 (B), 47 (BL), 49 (T), 50 (T), 51, 56 (BR), 64, 65, 66 (T), 69 (B), 70 (T), 71, 72 (B), 73 (T), 76, 79 (TL), 84 (B), 86 (T),88 (B), 92 (T), 98, 99, 100, 101, 102, 104 (B), 105, 106 (T), 107, 108, 109, 110 (B), 118 (B), 120 (L), 121 (T), 122 (B), 123 (B), 124 (B), 129 (T), 130 (TR), 132, 134 (TR), 137 (TL & BR), 141 (T), Back Cover (BL)

Michael Zagaris: Front Cover, 1, 4-5, 8, 12 (B), 21 (B), 22 (B), 24 (T), 27 (B), 30 (B), 31 (T), 32 (B), 33 (T), 35 (B), 41 (TR & BL), 42 (TL & TR), 43 (T), 44 (TL & TR), 45, 46 (BL & BR), 48, 49 (B), 58 (T), 66 (B), 67 (TL), 68, 69 (T), 72 (L & T), 77 (BL), 86 (BR), 87, 88 (T), 89 (T), 91, 92 (B), 93, 94, 104 (TR), 118 (T), 119, 120 (BR), 122 (T), 123 (TL & TR), 125 (T), 126, 133 (BL), 139 (CL & BR), 140 (T & C), Back Cover (TL & BCL)